OUR AMAZING WORLD
# DOLPHINS

Kay de Silva

*Aurora*

To my family with love & gratitude

# Contents

| | | | |
|---|---|---|---|
| Dolphins | 5 | Dolphin Families | 20 |
| Anatomy | 6 | Baby Dolphins | 21 |
| Habitat | 8 | Play | 22 |
| Migration | 9 | Intelligence | 24 |
| Breathing | 10 | Atlantic Spotted Dolphins | 26 |
| Sleeping | 11 | Bottlenose Dolphins | 27 |
| Feeding | 12 | Dusky Dolphins | 28 |
| Hunting | 14 | Pacific White-sided Dolphins | 29 |
| Echo-location | 15 | Risso's Dolphins | 30 |
| Dolphin Chatter | 16 | Amazon River Dolphins | 31 |
| Social Animals | 18 | Dolphins in Trouble | 32 |

*A pod of playful dolphins swimming over a coral reef.*

# Dolphins

Dolphins are *mammals* that live in the sea. They are very intelligent, playful, and friendly. They also love to show-off.

## Anatomy

Dolphins, like their close relatives whales, are not fish. However, they do have powerful bodies like fish. They use their tails to propel their way forward at top speeds.

The fin on their backs is called the *dorsal fin*. This fin gives dolphins a sense of direction and stability. Unlike most mammals, dolphins do not have hair on their bodies.

*A dolphin showing-off its powerful body.*

*There is plenty to eat on this coral reef.*

## Habitat

The place where an animal lives is called its *habitat*. There are dolphin habitats all around the world. Most dolphins live in oceans, while some are found in rivers.

*Dolphins travel many miles in search of new habitats.*

# Migration

Dolphins stay in places where there is plenty of food. During winter or when food is scarce, dolphins will go in search of food. They can travel hundreds of miles just to look for habitats that have food.

*A Humpback Dolphin surfacing in South Africa.*

# Breathing

Dolphins breathe air. They do not have gills like fish. Like whales, dolphins breathe through a *blowhole*, which is found on the top of their heads. They use this blowhole to draw in air, just like you use your nostrils.

*A dolphin at rest.*

# SLEEPING

Dolphins sleep for 16 hours each day. When dolphins sleep, they close just one eye, and half of their brain sleeps for 8 hours. When one side of their brain wakes up, the other side of their brain sleeps for another 8 hours. They can also swim while they are asleep. They can do this so they go up to the surface every now and then to breathe.

# Feeding

Dolphins are *carnivores*. They eat only meat. They feed on fish, squid, crab, and plankton. Some large dolphins eat smaller sea animals such as seals and sea turtles.

Dolphins do not use their teeth for chewing. Instead, they use their teeth to grab food, which they then swallow whole. Dolphins have two stomachs. One is used to store food, while the other is used for digestion.

*Who will grab this tasty treat?*

*A dolphin pod feeding.*

# Hunting

Dolphins are clever hunters. They sometimes hunt in groups. A group of dolphins surrounds a school of fish so that the fish form a dense shoal or group of fish. Each dolphin then takes a turn to dive into the shoal of fish and eat. They also sometimes catch bigger fish by hitting them with their tails.

*A dolphin uses echo-location to navigate the mysterious deep-sea.*

# Echo-location

Dolphins use *echo-location* to navigate and hunt. They make a clicking sound. When this sound wave hits an object, it bounces back. Dolphins listen to the echo. They use this to determine the size, shape, distance, speed, and direction of an object. Sometimes sound waves can enter the inside of an object, helping dolphins *look inside* a thing without actually seeing it.

## Dolphin Chatter

Dolphins talk to each other. They use different sounds, such as whistles and clicks, to communicate. Just like humans, they use facial expressions and gestures when they talk. Dolphins also communicate using bubble blowing, fin caresses, and jaw claps.

It is said that dolphins chat with other dolphins about all kinds of things, including how they are feeling. Sometimes when a dolphin is bullied by other dolphins, the bullied dolphin comes back the next day with friends to get back at the bullies.

*A cheeky dolphin sticking out its tongue.*

## Social Animals

Dolphins are social animals. A group of dolphins is called a *pod*. A dolphin pod usually has 2 to 40 members. Sometimes there could be hundreds in a single pod.

Within the group, dolphins protect each other. They depend on each other when hunting for food. They also form long-lasting friendships. When a pod of dolphins meets another pod of old friends, they have a greeting ceremony.

*Pod mates enjoying the sunset.*

*A family of dolphins swimming by.*

# Dolphin Families

Mother dolphins are called *cows*, and fathers are called *bulls*. Young dolphins are called *calves*. Baby dolphins grow inside their mothers for 12 months before they are born. At the birth, another female dolphin in the pod helps to deliver the calf.

*Mother and baby swimming together.*

# Baby Dolphins

Unlike other mammals, dolphins are born tail first. Calves can swim within minutes of being born. Mother dolphins sometimes whistle continuously to their babies for several days after their birth.

Baby dolphins drink their mother's milk for up to 18 months. They stay beside their mothers for as long as 6 years.

# Play

Dolphins love leaping out of the water into the air. This is called *breaching*. They breach to look for fish-eating birds and other signs of shoals of fish. Sometimes they breach to get rid of *parasites*. At times they breach to conserve energy. Most of the time, they breach just for fun.

Dolphins play with other dolphins. They play hide-and-seek in the seaweed and wrestle each other. They also play with other creatures, such as birds, turtles, and even human swimmers. They enjoy surfing on waves and breaching alongside boats.

*Happy surfers riding a wave.*

# INTELLIGENCE

Next to humans, dolphins are said to be the most intelligent of creatures. Relative to their size, they have one of the largest brains in the animal kingdom. They use tools such as sea sponges to cover themselves when they search for food at the bottom of the sea.

Dolphins in captivity easily learn new acrobatic tricks. They can also be creative and come up with their own tricks.

*A dolphin in training.*

*An Atlantic Spotted Dolphin leaping into the air.*

# Atlantic Spotted Dolphins

*Atlantic Spotted Dolphins* can often be seen in the Gulf Stream of the North Atlantic Ocean. They are mid-sized dolphins. Just like other dolphins, they enjoy having fun. They swim very fast and like doing acrobatic aerial displays.

*A pod of Bottlenose Dolphins performing tail-stands.*

# Bottlenose Dolphins

*Bottlenose Dolphins* have short, rounded snouts that look like bottles. They are the most common species of dolphins, and they can be found in almost all the oceans of the world. They like living along the coast, but sometimes they go deep into the ocean.

*A Dusky Dolphin playing at the Kaikoura Coast, New Zealand.*

# Dusky Dolphins

*Dusky Dolphins* are found in the Southern Hemisphere. These dolphins like staying in coastal areas and enjoy the cool currents of inshore waters. They are one of the smaller species of dolphins, and they are well known for their amazing acrobatics. They can perform different tricks as they breach.

*A Pacific White-sided Dolphin leaping out of the water.*

# Pacific White-sided Dolphins

*Pacific White-sided Dolphins* are found in the cool waters of the North Pacific Ocean. They are very energetic and active, and they like to socialize with other species of dolphins. They look out for approaching boats to show-off their breaching skills to people on board.

*A Risso's Dolphin and her calf.*

# Risso's Dolphins

*Risso's Dolphins* are the largest dolphin species. They are found in all the oceans but prefer deep tropical waters. The front parts of their bodies are bigger than the rest, and their tails are narrow. They are not as friendly as other dolphins. They rarely interact with humans.

Baby Risso's Dolphins are grey and sometimes brown. As they grow older, their bodies get darker, until they are almost completely black. As they grow older still, their color lightens again. Older Risso's Dolphins are almost completely white.

*Notice the Amazon River Dolphin's long "beak".*

# Amazon River Dolphins

*Amazon River Dolphins* live in freshwater rivers. They are also known as Pink Dolphins. These river dolphins can grow bigger than a human being. They can turn their heads 180 degrees. Unlike other dolphins, they do not have a dorsal fin. Instead, they have a hump on their backs. They also have a long beak.

*A beautiful dolphin dancing at dusk.*

# Dolphins in Trouble

*Global warming* and *pollution* have made it hard for dolphins to find suitable habitats. This causes dolphins to die of starvation. Caring for our *environment* will help protect dolphins and their habitats.

# Our Amazing World

## COLLECT THEM ALL

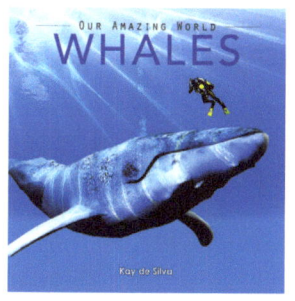   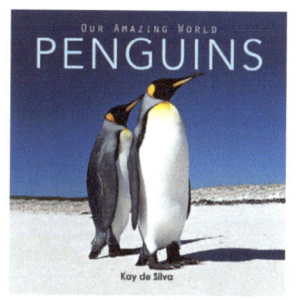

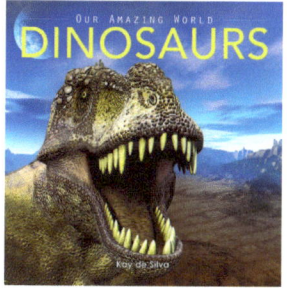  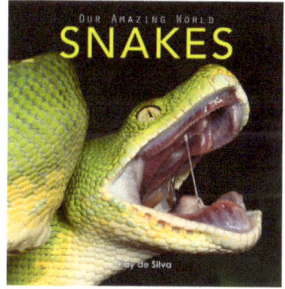 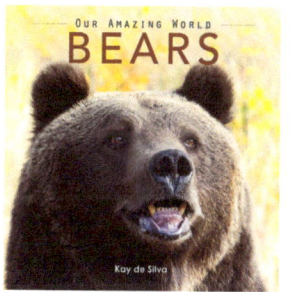

 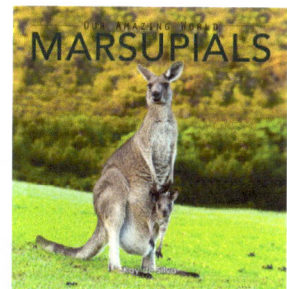

Aurora
An imprint of CKTY Publishing Solutions
28 Middle Road, Camberwell,
Victoria 3124, Australia

Text copyright © Kay de Silva, 2013
The moral right of the author has been asserted

A catalog record of the book is available from the National Library of Australia
ISBN: 978-0-9875970-2-1
All rights reserved

Front cover, 12-13, Alexander Cherednichenko/Shutterstock; 5, 8, 9, 20, 22-23, 32, Willyam Bradberry/Shutterstock; Back cover, Pannochka/Shutterstock; 1, Witthanya P/Shutterstock; 2-3, Anna Segeren/Shutterstock; 6-7, Tom C Amon/Shutterstock; 10, Brett Atkins/Shutterstock; 11, UgputuLFSS/Shutterstock; 14, Joe Stone/Shutterstock; 15, Ollyy/Shutterstock; 16-17, Four Oaks/Shutterstock; 18-19, Sad 444/Shutterstock; 21, Darryl Vest/Shutterstock; 24-25, Eelena Larina/Shutterstock; 26, Juan Gracie/Shutterstock; 27, Mike Price/Shutterstock; 28, Light & Magic Photography/Shutterstock; 29, Suzi Logan/Shutterstock; 30, Eric Isselee/Shutterstock; 31, Guentermanus/Shutterstock

Printed in the United States of America

www.ingramcontent.com/pod-product-compliance
Lightning Source LLC
Chambersburg PA
CBHW040020050426
42452CB00002B/66